WHO DOES NOT ENV

Maria Fusco is an award-winning working-class writer, born in Belfast and living in Scotland. Her interdisciplinary work spans the registers of critical, fiction and performance writing. Her work has been commissioned by bodies including: Artangel, BBC Radio 4, National Theatre Wales and supported by Arts Council England, Creative Scotland and the Royal Opera House. She is currently Professor of Interdisciplinary Writing at the University of Dundee, previously holding posts at the University of Edinburgh and Goldsmiths, University of London. mariafusco.net

Also by Maria Fusco

BOOKS

Nine Qwerty Bells: Fiction for Live Voice	(Whitechapel Gallery, 2019)
Give Up Art: Critical Writing	(New Documents, 2018)
Legend of the Necessary Dreamer	(Vanguard Editions, 2017)
Master Rock	(Book Works, 2015)
Gonda	(Sternberg Press, 2012)
The Mechanical Copula	(Sternberg Press, 2010)

PERFORMANCE WORKS

Mollspeak	(Museum of the Home, 2021)
ECZEMA!	(National Theatre Wales, 2018)
Master Rock	(Artangel and BBC Radio 4, 2015)

Who does not envy with us is against us
three essays on being working-class

Maria Fusco

Broken Sleep Books

ISBN: 978-1-915760-86-9

Cover designed by Aaron Kent

Edited & Typeset by Aaron Kent

Broken Sleep Books Ltd
Rhydwen
Talgarreg
Ceredigion
SA44 4HB

Broken Sleep Books Ltd
Fair View
St Georges Road
Cornwall
PL26 7YH

Contents

A Belly of Irreversibles

I was never allowed to tell people where I lived. This was because I lived in a bad area. Other things were classified as bad, but they were always plural. There was only one bad area: the one I lived in.

I now live in a good area. I am still working-class.

Sitting in a hotel breakfast room on Renfrew Street in Glasgow, I heard a loud ring tone rattling out from the kitchen, it was *The Sash*. I told the person I was with what I was hearing but they didn't understand so I had to explain what *The Sash* is and how it sickens and scares working-class Northern Irish Catholics of my generation. I was careful to keep my voice down, so the person in the kitchen with *The Sash* ringtone wouldn't hear me, wouldn't poison my breakfast, wouldn't try to kill me. I had completely lost my appetite. When the full Scottish fried breakfast (I had ordered before hearing *The Sash* ringtone) arrived I gulped down every scrap, so nothing went to waste. I was tempted to drink the milk in the little jug too, because it was free and that was what I used to be told to do when I was growing up, for the calcium. I did not do this because I was worried the person I was with (someone who I already knew well at that time, who is still infact a friend and who is also working-class) would judge me. I was calibrating what magnitude of working-class behaviour was acceptable and how working-class my friend was, compared to how working-class I was. I didn't want to disgrace myself.

When I went to primary school I could already read and count. My wonderful father had taught me; he was always unemployed (as were the majority the other men in the bad area) so he was about alot. The primary school class of thirty-three was divided into different reading groups, apparently according to aptitude. I was put into the lowest ability group because of the bad area I lived in. I knew this was unfair, for me and for the others, but I could not prove they could read, I could only prove I could read.

The first thing I want to know about people is what class they are. I don't believe in social mobility: you are always the same class as the one you grew up in even if your circumstances have radically changed. It is relatively easy in the UK to work out what class people are, if you've got the appetite for it. However, when you start working abroad (which if you've actioned your spiralling upwardly mobile aspirations well enough, then you will be) it is almost impossible that you are grasping the nuance of detectable signifiers of another country's class system. You simply cannot be as sure as you would like to be. This is actually a pretty constricting way to be in the world.

On the rare occasions I was offered a lift home from school by the mother of one of my middle-class schoolmates, I always had to tell them I lived in a different area, an area three tiers better than my own, but a working-class area nonetheless so I would appear credible. These mothers with cars, for it was never the fathers, would bring me to where I asked them to and then drop me off. I would wait until they had driven quite a way off, assuring them I was fine, and then I walked the long walk home. It would have been much quicker just to have walked straight back from school. I knew they knew I was lying because each mother only ever offered once and then never again. This made me feel ashamed. Ashamed I had to lie, but not ashamed about the bad area I lived in, because I knew this was not my fault.

One of my middle-class friends asked me to her house for dinner after one time. She lived quite far away from where the primary school was, but it was ok because there was a school bus that took the middle-class children to their area, there was of course no bus taking the working-class children to our area. I was very excited and, surely it goes without saying, also very nervous. Her whole family was sitting around a giant kitchen table in a kitchen, the table was basically the footprint of the lower floor of my whole house. Her mother served the father first, a great big slab of juicy looking steak, a mound of boiled potatoes with the skins on, and a pile of buttery cabbage. I'd never had steak before in real life, it looked really delicious. But, I was not served steak, I was served sausages. To be fair, everyone except the father was served sausages so I was not being deliberately left out. However, I was still extremely disappointed and could not understand why different members of the family got different food, and why the father had been served first. In my house, children were always fed first, were given the best bits of the cheap food we had, the parents took the scraps. The implication being: our children will die if they are not fed. Families in the bad area I grew up in fed all children this way, not just their own.

I note how often other writers evoke a relatively well-known Greek myth to lend gravity and longitudinal context to their subject. You'll start noticing it too, now that I've drawn your attention to it, you probably have already anyway, maybe you even like it, sometimes I like it myself actually. I try to summon a Greek myth to dance teasingly in this text (like the woman from the opening credits of *Tales of the Unexpected*) to give my subject the dignity I think it deserves. Sisyphus immediately comes to mind, because… well you know… it's obvious. Prometheus, I have a fancy for the raging symbolism of fire and the image of his luscious regenerating liver. Antigone's moral grandeur seduces then mocks me with its completeness.

The working-class way is fragmentary and composed of glittery remnants: Harp lager can ring pulls, shattered glass, pearlescent phlegm streaked with blood.

The rest of that day in Glasgow I kept thinking about the leftover milk in the little jug in the hotel breakfast room, of it being poured down the sink: the awful waste.

I had an argument with a friend once about innate cultural value. I gave the example of how *Metal Mickey* is as important as *Jules et Jim* because, I said, it has to do with the analytical eye you are casting over the content, not the content itself. I knew my example was facetious and a wee bit silly but I really felt it. I still really feel it. I chose *Jules et Jim* rather than another more obscure and probably interesting film to me (even when I was child) like say *Come and See* or *Themroc* or *Shellshock Rock* because I thought they would have been more likely to have seen *Jules et Jim*, so yes, I was sort of patronising them. They snorted, I mean they literally snorted with derision.

Taste is actually quite easy to learn.

It was only when I started mixing with middle-class people I realised drinking excessive amounts of alcohol can bloat you. The neighbours I had grown up beside in the bad area (mainly men, the ones who drank excessive amounts of alcohol, most did not) were emptied out by it. There was nothing left of them. I never questioned where they got the money to buy the drink, I didn't know how much drink cost anyway.

A friend told me about someone they know who used to get a raw jelly cube in their school lunchbox as a sweet treat. They told me this because they were trying to explain how poor the other person was. They were trying to be nice. They also told me because, well let's face it, it is a funny image: bouncy. I laughed to be polite and because, as I've just said there, it is quite amusing. But what I was really thinking was: I would rather have had a raw jelly cube than a free school dinner.

I probably don't need to tell you here about the necessity and the indignity of free school dinners. All you need to know, incase you don't already, is that the tickets for free school dinners were a different colour than the tickets for ordinary school dinners.

I am disgusted and overwhelmed by the idea of wastefulness, yet I think I waste a lot of my time. I think this is because my time feels like it costs nothing. I am my own resource. I use myself. I wear myself out. I'm doing it now, for you, on this page.

I. I. I. I. I was introducing the guest film I had selected to be shown at a festival when, standing at the mic just about to speak, it occurred to me, that what I am really interested in is working-classness as method.

If you've grown up very poor working-class, it's relatively straightforward to describe the slight portions of poverty (the half full milk jug, the jelly cube, and yes, they are often calibrated by food, I mean, honest to god, how could they not be) but it's so very hard to explain the essential distinctiveness of working-classness and how it burrows under your nails. I bite my nails so I am speaking figuratively but it does feel like a burrowing, like a *ceremony*.

Into the mic I said: What I am really interested in is working-classness as method. I was surprised it came out. Afterwards, quite a lot of people came up to me, asking, in a genuine way, what I meant by working-classness as method. All I wondered was: Why are they so fucking interested?

Tantalus, I should have summoned Tantalus!

And I return to this question regularly. What does working-classness as method actually mean? And who cares about it, apart from people like me. And again, I'm here with it now, in this text, clattering the tin bones of being working-class. How you go about things; how you imagine something will turn out; the expectant emotion of change; wanting but never being sure.

I told my mother about *The Sash* ringtone incident in Glasgow. I told her because I had little else to talk with her about and was trying to fill time on the telephone. Her voice was stiff: a fatal mix of indignation and incomprehension. Did you give them your real name? Yes, of course I'd given them my real name, I had to, I'd been invited to give a public lecture. Why? But why did you give them your real name? She was trying to be helpful. But what else could I have done, hadn't I been invited to be *myself.*

Why I write the way I write (Sally)

All I did was watch tv. I am not sure how I came to writing. I didn't read books when I was growing up. I was not bookish. When I peruse interviews with other writers, they often cite their joy of reading, their pleasure in getting lost in the complete universe of a text. I was busy watching gory horror films, ultra-violent video nasties and soft porn. I enjoyed getting lost in these because the extreme happenings in them came to an end, whereas the extreme happenings in my everyday life, in working-class Belfast during the very worst of the Troubles, were cyclical and brutalising.

btw, if you are wondering how I was able to watch gory horror films, ultra-violent video nasties and soft porn on tv since I can remember it's because I basically didn't have any parental guidance or supervision. All I did was watch tv, sat up by myself watching these gory horror films, ultra-violent video nasties and soft porn as often as they were on, while everyone else (there were six of us in the tiny terrace house, I was by far the youngest) was in bed. All I can say is that aggressively militarised environment of violent civil unrest does funny things to adults.

Back to this question of coming to writing. Whilst I *think* I feel writing is an intrinsic part of my identity (it has taken me ages to realise this, despite having been a writer for quite a long time) I've always been sure that being from Belfast definitely is: I am sodden with the city's words, I was surrounded by plenty of these, understanding their immense power, in a shy, inchoate way, for example, there was always plenty of words written on walls, in English and in Irish. But mainly my relationship with the power of words was predicated on keeping your mouth shut, pretending you did not know something in school, not talking over the turned-up volume on the tv and never ever stating a preference of any sort or asking anybody for anything.

Here's something that you probably don't know, you might well find it interesting: when you are inside your house and there is a riot or yet another terrifying and thrilling peak of civil unrest is happening outside, you experience it through sound. You stay well clear of windows for at least two good reasons: firstly, you don't want to be seen witnessing anything and secondly, you are hiding behind a wall further back in the house so that if a bullet or a Saracen or a hijacked bus smashes through the front window it won't hit you directly. Because houses in bad areas are poorly made, the walls are thin, even the one at the back you are hiding behind. You hear nearly everything and each sound you hear has a diacritical relationship to the others: you are learning.

I hardly never went out, except to school until I became a truant. All I did was watch tv.

When I made my First Confession, as all seven-year old Catholics across Northern Ireland did, I had nothing to confess, so naturally I lied. I'm sure this was not uncommon but I didn't know this at the time and certainly would not have admitted to any of my classmates I lied in Confession. I told the priest I said 'bad words' inside, to myself. I did not need to explain to the priest what bad words were, but for the avoidance of doubt here, when I said bad words when I was seven, I meant 'cunt', 'fuck' and oddly, 'turd'. I can't remember what penance the priest gave me, but I do remember being surprised he wasn't surprised I said bad words, and I was thankful for that.

Now, four very important words. In Belfast, during The Troubles, British soldiers were known as The Brits and the Royal Ulster Constabulary were known as The Peelers: thereby corralling two heavily armed, aggressive (and, in retrospect, probably terrified) security forces into manageable definite articles.

Like all families in our bad area, we bought *An Phoblacht*, a Republican newspaper which was sold door-to-door. After a quick read through (because if a particular neighbour happened to ask you a question about *An Phoblacht*'s contents you needed to have some sort of answer) we burnt it on the open fire in our living room. Burn after reading. We did this in case the Brits when they were raiding our house, as they did at least once a week (usually a Saturday morning when *Swap Shop* was on the tv) saw we had a copy, they would associate this with being an active Republican and would therefore punish us; that's what we thought we would happen anyway, it happened to other families in our street and surrounding streets all the time. Let me tell you, it is astonishing how immense the material volume of a small terrace house expands to when the interior is ripped apart and dumped on the street.

So, my respect of the power of words, well I blame my Mother, Sally. She had the most refined and deadly palette of insults I have ever, ever heard. Most are too serious, too personal for inclusion here, but I will share my very favourite with you

stick yer nose up my hole

For those of you who may not be *au fait* with what 'hole' means, it means arsehole, or asshole if you're reading this in North America.

Recently I heard on the radio that vultures wait until the carcasses they want to eat reach a highly advanced state of decay, then work their way in through the dead animal's hole, as an easy route to the soft insides. I am also remembering reading an historical account of a Catholic soldier who, on the cusp of being executed by a firing squad, requested to be shot in the hole, so his body would remain intact and he would not be denied access to heaven because he was incomplete. It was well known, even to me when I was growing up, that prisoners, including those who were our neighbours, smuggled goods of various sorts (including, amazingly, a tiny radio transmitter) up their holes, a poetic process named 'bangling'. All three of these examples strike me as good uses for a hole. Of course, I can think of others, as I am sure you probably can too.

Figuratively,

stick yer nose up my hole

is kinetically sophisticated and perversely sensual. It demands a lyrical form of surrender, of disciplinary sublimation, through the abrasive enactment of a complicated and highly specific sort of [meta]physical positioning to carry it out. It assumes obedience and therefore presupposes consent. It is almost jargon.

It's important to remember, to visualise even, when one sticks something into something that is gooey, gummy, moist (let's say a hole for example) the chances are the thing that has been stuck in

19

(let's say a nose for example) will still be smeared with residue upon removal. Accordingly, Sally's words adhere: her insult has legacy.

I have never once insulted Sally, to her face anyway. Despite being daily assaulted, ambushed and amused by her own relentless charivari, I would never dream of saying a bad word in front of her. Firstly, I'm certain I would not be able to live up to the sophistication of her lurid missiles, so if I tried it would only be dilution. Secondly, I was brought up by Sally to be polite, to always put others' feelings first, somewhat ironic given what I've just been telling you about her. Even in the face of unfairness, aggression and baiting, I am still inclined to be like this today, an aspect of myself that I value to a point but that also really pisses me off.

I'm not sure, and to be honest I have no way of ever finding out if anyone did in fact ever stick their nose up Sally's hole. This further leads me to wonder now if I would like someone to stick their nose up my hole, I think I might, I may give it a go after finishing writing this. Obviously, neither of these last two ponderances are the point here. The point is Sally's atavistic demand for degradation, for subservience through baroque biological configuration, for mucilaginous power. The point is, that a working-class woman of her generation, like Sally, was indeed almost completely powerless.

Sally often used to refer to herself in the third person present tense, for example "Sally takes herself up to the shops…" positioning herself, with persuasive immediacy, as the main character in her own life. And because Sally was using the third person present tense, the affect was one of an omniscient narrator, who confidently penetrates all characters in her directorial panorama (minor, major and all those in between) thereby asserting comprehension and control, on her part. I wasn't the only one who watched a lot of tv. She was assembling herself through a combative miasma of actions and characteristics which, from a distance, lent her sovereignty. This is what I think she thought, the bit about sovereignty I mean, not what I thought: I thought she was dissembling.

Actually, when you look at it, Sally referring to herself in the third person is not dissimilar to seven-year-old me watching gory horror films, ultra-violent video nasties and soft porn on tv: we were both trying to find a point of resolution.

For a sizeable portion of my life, I believed Sally was unique in the privation and anguish she experienced as a working-class woman. I believed this because Sally encouraged, well I might as well be honest, indoctrinated me to. I also believed it because I never met anyone in my adult, working life whose mother (or father) had led the life that Sally had. I still haven't. I have worked with people who said they were working-class but went away on holidays once a year, ate out in restaurants on birthdays, owned a car, got more than one Christmas present, even one person whose parents had had a cleaner. My Mother cleaned hospitals for a meagre living, poor people can barely afford cleaning products let alone cleaners. I can't in good faith say that these people were not working-class but they were not my kind of working-class.

I continue carry the melancholia and implication of the rubbishness of Sally's life, even though I now know her experience was quite average for thousands, millions of women of her social standing. The harm these women endured lowered them in their own eyes. Whilst shame is both a noun and a verb, collective shame is servitude.

I also now realise that even though Sally's life (and indeed my own life growing up) was extremely shite, it was not as bad as others' lives, not nearly as half as bad at all. I struggle with the small portion of privilege the era I grew up in afforded me (I got to study at university for free) it wounds me and it really fucking pisses me off.

The only thing marking out Sally's experience from millions of other working-class women, is that she lived through The Troubles, hence her carrying a dismembered head into the house and putting it into the bath with the frozen Christmas turkey to keep the head fresh because The Peelers wouldn't let an ambulance through. One of many, many gruesome vignettes. And no, the turkey didn't get eaten despite being sealed in plastic because Sally was very particular about food hygiene. She threw it out, the waste nearly killed her.

Sally had her tarnished and tiring life, a tourniquet of poverty and war, but I like to think at least she had her words.

I showed a longform piece of fiction I was working on to another, more experienced, writer. One chapter contained an edited transcript of a tape-recording of my family from 1980. The writer spoke with passion about the formal beauty of a short passage in which Sally relates an incident about cleaning the chapel in the hospital she was working in and accidently putting all the candles out. The writer did not know it was a transcription until I told her. I was so proud knowing that those words, the very best words, were verbatim Sally.

Whilst I was writing this essay it had a different ending, an ending where Sally was still alive. Eighty-eight years old, slowly starving herself in a residential care home in North Belfast, having somehow survived Covid in a place where two thirds of residents had died of it. During the four years Sally lived in the home, she mostly enjoyed the company of the other woman there, unaware that nearly all the women were middle-class and Protestant; she might well have felt differently about them if she had.

And the reason why I wrote about Sally in the past tense, even though she was not yet dead, was because I thought she had already lost the use of her skilfully obscene and devastatingly contemptuous words, because she was uprooted, out of place. Her words had no target. By this I mean, for example, she no longer needed to protect her heavily pregnant body, and the soft skulled mass within, from being prodded by Brits with rifles whilst spreadeagled against a yard wall for hours in a bitter Belfast December. What would you do in her shoes, not to show weakness? And, incase you are wondering, yes, of course I was the wet body inside Sally's body.

A very old working-class woman in the last few days of her life is lying in narrow bed in a hot room in a residential care home. It is first thing in the morning. The care assistant tells the woman's daughters they can go into her room, the big light is on, the wall-mounted tv is blasting. The old woman is sleeping. Her daughters wake her gently by stroking her hands. They know this is the last time they will see her alive. The woman wakes up slowly, confused, she cannot understand why she is still in bed, she struggles to rise but has no strength. The daughters feel guilty they have been so selfish waking her, wanting to speak with her, thinking they should have let her continue to drift. The woman is distraught, she's worried she'll be late for work.

I've deliberately chosen not to employ any references here because I didn't want to shortcut with the words of others. But there is one quotation I want to give you, from Saint Augustine's *Confessions*, "You are so high among the highest, and I am low among the lowest, a mean thing. You never go away from us. Yet we have difficulty in returning to you." These words are the closest, most direct address to the condition of being from a poor working-class Belfast background that I can offer. And I do love these words, but not as much as

stick yer nose up my hole

for Sally Fusco (1933-2021)

Who does not envy with us
is against us

I was sitting in a bar with a group of university colleagues, one of them got up to go to the toilet trampling over my coat because it was the easiest route for him to get to the toilet. I remember this, I know he will not.

I suspect envy is a mood, rather than an emotion. If envy is a mood, then it is pursuant, in constant need of *the* appropriate mark, for without the slimmest possibility of wounding and then consuming its quarry surely envy can't exist: this mood has teeth.

Understanding envy as a mood is helpful for thinking around class because of its ambient, atavistic nature. I will rename it envy mood, for precision. In the midst of envy mood every single mark, not one nor two nor ten nor one million billion trillion specific marks count, it's the entire universe of human gain, breath, activity, multiplication, entropy that working-class people, like me (perhaps only me, I can't be sure) simply cannot fathom. Nothing we own is inherited, so, no jewellery, no glassware, no furniture, no books, no artworks, no land.

It is often observed informally that envy is concealed admiration (I haven't fully made up my mind about this but I think it's incorrect) if this is the case then envying every single mark - known, unknown and indeed probably unknowable - would lack gravity, leaving the one in envy mood turning inside out and outside in, flailing in perpetual and futile motion, writhing slippy in unproductive atopic labour: an empty used condom discarded due to fatigue.

I used to co-teach with a fairly eminent philosopher who would bring four Upper Crust baguettes into the university seminar room at the beginning of a day's teaching, all the same filling. He would eat the baguettes before and during teaching, but not after. At the time I didn't understand why or how he could possibly eat, or more accurately require, four Upper Crust baguettes but now I'm wondering if the baguettes were, to him, a necessary condition of being able to be who he was whilst inside the university. Spending a day teaching, hours' worth of transmogrifying immaterial notions into material bites, swallowing, digesting, and yes ultimately shitting out the four Upper Crust baguettes into the toilet next door to the seminar room. He was often in the toilet for quite long periods of time, whilst students queued outside waiting patiently to use it.

Much theoretical writing around envy states social proximity to the subject of envy is key, that envy develops only amongst equals. Such writing insists you cannot envy that which you have not seen or physically interacted with. This would mean the one experiencing envy mood wishes to be the same and to do the same as its mark, to camouflage. Consider the snow hare's seasonal change of coat colour, white in winter to brown in summer, if the hares are even a wee bit out of sync with the season the hare's mismatched camouflage is fatal. I do not agree with this idea of envy and proximity: envy requires imagination.

I lived in London for more than twenty years. It took me at least five years to realise that when people shoved me aside to get on the Tube in rush hour it was not because they didn't see me, it was because they *chose* not to see me. In some ways I am slow a learner, and in some ways I am too polite. I suspect some people mistake politeness for weakness, maybe it's just easier to be rude to other people and then pretend it shows strength.

My envy mood is not to begrudge the entitlement others seem to possess, I do not, 'seem' is the key word here for I have no idea what others really possess. When I read the eighteenth-century term for the middle class was the middling class it made so much sense to me. A class that is *trying*. So, perversely, this envy mood, its leitmotif, welcomes not only those who envy what they never had or perhaps never even witnessed, moreover, envy mood also welcomes those who, arguably, have no right to envy, those who've already had too much.

I feel sure a proportion of the middling class mete out their envy mood in vexed response to the traditionally underprivileged doing well, or to use old money 'making something of themselves'.

Our envy mood is roused by the middling classes' confidence in expressing their envy of us. They have absolutely no compunction in their gaudy display, no apparent grace. This drains all social pleasure and value. Sense of worth isn't a skin that's given, it's grown through ongoing interactions with others. And how does this play put in a real-life social context? They triangulate with their own kind, skilfully becoming engrossed in a very important and serious conversation, simply turning away from us, a slightly degree at a time, geometrically excising us from their field of vision, parsing a possible *network* with surgical social precision. In this moment, the net is for us, the work is for them.

Occasionally the middling classes appear to show mercy, casting their net. We dither, deciphering the validity of the bait can be very confusing, one element of us (the stomach maybe) wants to be part of whatever it is they are part of, another element (the spleen maybe) believing it to be a trap, tries to flee. There are many socially acceptable ways to flee, here's a few examples in alphabetical order: disassociation; excessive alcohol consumption; hiding in a locked toilet cubicle; hiding in a kitchen; hypochondria; laughing extremely loudly when you don't find what you are laughing at funny; making yourself useful to others like for example taking it upon yourself, without being explicitly asked, to offer a bowl of crisps around the whole group; self-depreciation; resignation.

A few years ago, I was asked to judge a highly prestigious and economically elephantine literary prize. I agreed because it got me a free transatlantic flight, accommodation, a fee and thirty free books, and because I was flattered to be asked. Actually, I should tell you I was asked to both be a judge and to chair my fellow judges, so I was doing two things whilst they were only doing one. The thing I want to share with you is that the prize was, and is still, not technically open to writers who hold permanent academic positions, who are perceived to be in the position of stable wealth and who therefore do not need the prize money. In reality, of course, this rule did not seem to have been rigorously enforced. Infact, two of the very worthy and utterly brilliant (I'm not just saying this to take the bad look of myself, they really are) writers who won that year's prize held tenured university positions, as indeed do I. My suggestion to the prize's director was that not all people who teach at universities do so solely for the pleasure and, yes sometimes the privilege, of teaching, some of them also do it for money. I am one of these people.

Another, more fiscal, way to apprehend net work is to see what pittance is left after all other expenses have been deducted by the middling classes, the price of four Upper Crust baguettes for example. As I'm sure you'll know already, net income is the gross profit minus all other expenses. Which good jobs are left for us after they've all been picked over? This is our net work: what is left and how it has been chosen for us. It is about you, not for you.

If you've ever been at a work event with a buffet-type dining arrangement, you'll know exactly what I mean. All of the best food will have gone by the time you get to the table because you will have positioned yourself back towards the end of the queue so as not to look hungry.

I used to believe intelligence was aligned to how quickly a person grasped a concept, I suppose I'm still slightly of this mind. Where I grew up people didn't run (unless they were being chased by members of the security forces) but they were always walking very quickly, with an apparently strong sense of purpose, even though they were going nowhere specific and often nowhere at all. I often eat really quickly, gulping down food in hazardous chunks. Only now whilst writing this paragraph, I've realised, I do this because I am worried someone will take the food away from me.

The middling classes envy mood is highly sensitised to the acceleration of the social attainment of others and achingly attentive to the duration of their own attainment. They are dedicated. Duration is crucial here in more than one way. If the envy mood is dampened by the prolonged feeling of guilt of being envious then it's necessary to know, to acknowledge you are actually envious. My point here is, even in my careful and prolonged observation of the middling classes (I've spent my entire adult life with them) I cannot one hundred percent verify whether they don't know they are envious, or whether they know fine rightly but are pretending not to, because they just don't give a shit about working-class people. I think it's more likely the later. Members of the working classes witness this impiety on a daily basis, from tiny disrespectful violences such as the old university colleague trampling my coat I told you about at the start of this essay insignificant of course, to different coloured tickets for free dinners, to shite housing, to the amoral intersectional systemic pillorying, harassment and banditry done to poor working-class people.

The envy mood clatters and praises what is mediocre yet stays deadly silent about what is good. Silence being imposed not desired; silence being injurious. Clearly I'm not the first person to have articulated this tendency, but it's important to point out here because it destroys hope. And destroying hope irrevocably damages the material viability of economically poor communities.

I'm aware as I write this that I'm feeling anxious about coming across as angry. I worry there might be repercussions, I might be further triangulated out of a very important and serious conversation. Well you know, I am angry. I used to describe my anger as frustration until someone I trusted corrected me: frustration is anger, but wearing a nicer jacket. They told me the first bit about frustration being anger, I've added the second bit about the jacket myself because I think it works as an image and now I'm telling you because I want to you to see I'm quite good at conjuring images, don't forget, when I was growing up all I did was watch tv, I can't help but try to please you.

Now, I'm also quite good at asking questions. Here's two great ones: When will there be a ceasefire of envy mood's identity-negating violence? When will we be free?

Afterword

You will have noticed by now the proliferation of my use of first person past tense. Mostly in relaying an anecdote, a meaningful anecdote, a meaningful anecdote to illustrate what I consider to be an important point, I don't want to waste your time. I too have noticed that the majority of essayistic texts I've read by other working-class writers use first person past tense. Looks like we feel we need to be clear about our authenticity, to let you know this all really happened, to witness, to give testimony: to let you know, this isn't even the bloody half of it.

Acknowledgments

Early versions of two essays in this book have been previously published:

'A Belly of Irreversibles' was commissioned for Sean Edwards' artist's book *un un un un un un* to accompany the tour of his Wales in Venice 2019 exhibition *Undo Things Done*. Published by the Bluecoat and distributed by Cornerhouse Publications (2021)

'Why I write the way I write (Sally)', originally titled 'A Belfast Woman', was commissioned by the MAC in Belfast as part of its NINOW100 programme of new work responding to the one hundredth anniversary of the partition of Ireland and the creation of Northern Ireland as a state: https://themaclive.com/watch-listen ninow100 (2021)

Thanks to:
James Brook
Centre Culturel Irlandais, Paris
Sean Edwards
Aaron Kent
Simon Magill
Craig Martin
Marie-Anne Quay
and working-class writers everywhere

LAY OUT YOUR UNREST